The One True Church

by John Isaac Edwards and Larry R. Ping II

ONE STONE
BIBLICAL RESOURCES

Published by:
One Stone Press
979 Lovers Lane
Bowling Green, KY 42103

Printed in the United States of America

ISBN-13: 978-1-941422-48-9

www.onestone.com

Table of Contents

Identity of the One True Church

Welcome to this special series of Bible lessons concerning *the one true church!* Most people have misconceptions about what the church is. The Bible defines and describes the church. Thus, we look to the Bible to find out about the one true church.

Use of the word "church"

The word "church" appears 74 times in the New King James Version. It is first used by Jesus in Matthew 16:18: "I will build My church, and the gates of Hades shall not prevail against it." The English word "church" comes from the Greek word *ekklesia.* The basic meaning is the "called out."

1. A calling out of: "from *ek*, out of, and *klesis*, a calling" (*Vine's Expository Dictionary of New Testament Words*, p. 83).

2. Called out or forth; an assembly: "called out or forth...an assembly" (*Thayer's Greek-English Lexicon*, pp. 195-196).

This word is used four ways in the New Testament:

1. Congregation of the Israelites. "This is he who was in the _____ in the wilderness" (Acts 7:38). See Hosea 11:1.

2. Assembly of a riotous mob. "Some therefore cried one thing and some another, for the _____ was confused, and most of them did not know why they had come together....And when he had said these things, he dismissed the _____" (Acts 19:32, 41).

Memory Verse

And He put **all things** under His feet, and gave Him to be **head** over all things to the **church**, which is His **body**, the **fullness** of Him who fills all in all.

- Ephesians 1:22-23

3. Assembly of a body of citizens to discuss affairs of the state. "But if you have any other inquiry to make, it shall be determined in the lawful _____" (Acts 19:39).

4. The "called of Jesus Christ" (Romans 1:6). It is composed of those called to be _____ (Romans 1:7; 1 Corinthians 1:2); called in _____ _____ (Colossians 3:15); called unto _____ (1 Thessalonians 4:7); called out of _____ into _____ (1 Peter 2:9-10); called by the _____ (2 Thessalonians 2:14). This is the body of people over which Christ is Head and of which He is Savior (Ephesians 5:23).

As applied to the called of Jesus Christ, the word "church" is used two ways:

1. Universally—to designate all the saved everywhere

2. Locally—to designate the saved at a particular location

And I also say to you that you are Peter, and on this **rock** I will build My **church**, and the gates of Hades **shall not prevail** against it.

- Matthew 16:18

Identify which way the word "church" is used in the following passages, universally or locally:

1. Matthew 16:18 _____

2. 1 Corinthians 1:2 _____

3. Galatians 1:22 _____

4. Ephesians 1:22 _____

5. Ephesians 5:25 _____

6. Philippians 1:1 _____

7. Colossians 1:18 _____

8. 1 Thessalonians 1:1 _____

Identity Exercise

We learn what the church is from the passages in which the word is used. Please look up the Scriptures and fill in the blanks to learn the identity of the church:

It was _____ by _____ (Matthew 16:18); it can _____ and _____ (Matthew 18:17); the Lord _____ the _____ to it (Acts 2:47); _____ came upon it (Acts 5:11); it was _____ (Acts 8:1, 3); it has _____ (Acts 11:22); it _____ (Acts 11:22); it _____ (Acts 12:5); there were _____ and _____ in it (Acts 13:1); _____ were ordained in it (Acts 14:23); it was _____ _____ (Acts 14:27); it _____ (Acts 15:4); it was _____ (Acts 18:22); it can be _____ and was _____ with the blood of Christ (Acts 20:28); it can be _____ (Romans 16:5); it can _____ (Romans 16:23); _____ can be given to it (1 Cor. 10:32); it can be _____ (1 Corinthians 11:22); God _____ some in it (1 Corinthians 12:28); it can be _____ (1 Corinthians 14:4-5, 12); it can _____ (1 Corinthians 16:19); it makes known God's _____ _____ (Ephesians 3:10); _____ is given to God in it (Ephesians 3:21); Christ is the _____ and _____ of it (Ephesians 5:23); it is _____ to Christ (Ephesians 5:24); Christ _____ it and gave _____ for it (Ephesians 5:25); it should be _____ and without _____ (Ephesians 5:27); it _____ (Philippians 4:15); men _____ for it (Colossians 1:24); it can be taken _____ of (1 Timothy 3:5); it is the _____ of God, the _____ and _____ of the _____ (1 Timothy 3:15); it can be _____ (1 Timothy 5:16); its number is _____ in _____ (Hebrew 12:23); it was _____ unto (3 John 9).

WORD BANK

Christ	gather together	pillar	edified	blemish	greet
built	fear	ground	manifold wisdom	appoints	greet
spoken to	registered	subject	teachers	Savior	receives
speak	truth	purchased	prophets	loved	greeted
written	glory	ears	persecuted	Himself	greeted
despised	head	sends	prays	care	suffer
offended	overseen	added	spotless	house	Heaven
elders		saved		shares	burdened

> Jesus answered, "My **kingdom** is not of this **world**. If My kingdom were of this world, My **servants** would **fight**, so that I should not be delivered to the **Jews**; but now My kingdom is **not from here**."
>
> - John 18:36

Figures by which the church is made known

1. The kingdom of God. Jesus told Peter, "I will build My church...And I will give you the keys of the _____" (Matthew 16:18-19). Show from the Scriptures that the kingdom is the church and has been established. _____
   _____
   _____
   _____

   Name some things that are necessary to make a kingdom. _____
   _____
   _____
   _____

   What is the nature of the kingdom (John 18:36; Romans 14:17; Luke 17:20-21)? _____
   _____
   _____

   The kingdom parables reveal the identity of the church. Read Matthew 13 and be prepared to discuss what the kingdom is like. How does one enter the kingdom (John 3:5)? _____
   _____

   What did the Lord say about a kingdom divided against itself (Mark 3:24)? _____
   _____

2. The body of Christ. The _____ is the _____ (Ephesians 1:22-23) and the _____ is the _____ (Colossians 1:18, 24). How many bodies are there (Romans 12:4-5; Ephesians 4:4)? _____
   List three things that are in the body of Christ (Colossians 3:15; Ephesians 2:16; 5:23; Acts 2:47). _____
   _____

What is the relationship between Christ and the body (Colossians 1:18; Ephesians 1:21-23; 5:23)?

_____

_____

Read 1 Corinthians 12:12-27. What do you learn about the body from this reading? _____

_____

_____

Every part must _____ (Ephesians 4:16).

3. The house of God. Paul wrote Timothy, "but if I am delayed, I write so that you may know how you ought to conduct yourself in the _____ of God which is the _____ of the living God" (1 Timothy 3:15). What is meant by the term "house" (Luke 1:27; Acts 10:2; Hebrews 11:7)? _____

Outstanding features of God's house/family include: God is the _____ (Matthew 23:9; Ephesians 4:6). Christ is a _____ over the house (Hebrews 3:6). Christians are His _____ (Hebrews 2:11-12). Those in Christ are the _____ of God (Galatians 3:26-27); "_____ and _____" (2 Corinthians 6:18). "And if children, then _____—heirs of God and joint heirs with Christ" (Romans 8:17).

4. The temple of God. "Temple" suggests a place where God meets those who worship Him— temple built by Solomon (2 Chronicles 7:12-16). The church is God's spiritual temple today (1 Corinthians 3:9, 16-17; Ephesians 2:19-22). Who is the foundation of this temple (Isaiah 28:16; 1 Corinthians 3:11; Ephesians 2:20; 1 Peter 2:5-8)?

_____

Who are the stones (Ephesians 2:19-22; 1 Peter 2:5-10)? _____

For no other **foundation** can anyone lay than that which is laid, which is **Jesus Christ**.

- 1 Corinthians 3:11

> All the **nations** will be **gathered** before Him, and He will **separate** them one from another, as a **shepherd** divides his **sheep** from the **goats**.
>
> - Matthew 25:32

5. The bride of Christ. To the saints at Rome Paul said, "Therefore, my brethren, you also have become dead to the law through the body of Christ, that you may be _____ to another—to Him who was raised from the dead" (Romans 7:4). Paul wrote the church at Corinth, "For I am jealous for you with godly jealousy. For I have _____ you to one _____ that I may present you as a chaste virgin to Christ" (2 Corinthians 11:2). In his letter to the Ephesians, Paul talked about the husband/wife relationship and said, "I speak concerning _____ and the _____" (Ephesians 5:32). What do you learn about the church from this figure? _____

_____

6. The flock of God. Jesus often used the figure of sheep in His teaching. He warned of "false prophets, who come to you in _____ clothing" (Matthew 7:15). When He saw the multitudes, He said they were "like _____ having no _____" (Matthew 9:36). He sent His apostles "to the lost _____ of the house of Israel... as _____ in the midst of wolves" (Matthew 10:6, 16). The judgment is depicted "as a shepherd divides his _____ from the goats" (Matthew 25:32). Luke 15:4-6 is the parable of _____. Read John 10:1-30. The Lord told Peter, "_____ my _____" (John 21:15-17). The New Testament church is represented as the flock of God. The Lord's disciples are His sheep (Acts 20:28-29; 1 Peter 5:3). Who is the Shepherd (John 10:11; Hebrews 13:20; 1 Peter 5:4)? _____

_____

7. The vineyard of the Lord. What is the kingdom like (Matthew 20:1-16)?

_____

Read Matthew 21:28-31. Observe the following: the relationship:
"_____"; the call: "go _____"; the day:
"_____; the place: "in my _____." Read
Matthew 21:33-46. What do you learn from the parable of the wicked
vine growers? _____

_____

1 Corinthians 3:9 reads, "For we are God's fellow _____; you
are God's _____." Notice the exhortation in 1 Corinthians 15:58.

Understanding what the church is, we are now in a better position to learn
what the Bible teaches about the one true church.

Some questions from our study

1. Write a sentence telling what the church of Christ is. _____

_____

_____

2. Tell how the word "church" is used in the New Testament. _____

_____

3. What are the figures by which the church is known? _____

_____

_____

Lesson 2

Origin of the One True Church

There are many theories about when the church, the kingdom of God, was established. It's been said: The church was established before the foundation of the world; it began in the garden of Eden; it had its beginning in the days of Abraham; it began during the mission of John the Baptist, and/or during the personal ministry of Jesus; it began on the day of Pentecost in Acts 2; it has not yet been established. This study takes a spiritual look at how, when, and where the one true church began as revealed on the pages of the word of God.

The church originated with God

The Holy Spirit revealed, "and to make all see what is the fellowship of the mystery, which from the beginning of the ages has been hidden in God who created all things through Jesus Christ; to the intent that now the manifold wisdom of God might be made known by the _____ to the principalities and powers in the heavenly places, according to the eternal purpose which He purposed in Christ Jesus our Lord" (Ephesians 3:9-11). What do you learn about the origin of the church from this statement?

_____

_____

_____

The church originated in the last days

Isaiah prophesied, "Now it shall come to pass in the _____ _____ that the mountain

Memory Verse

To the intent that now the manifold **wisdom** of God might be made known by the **church** to the principalities and **powers** in the **heavenly places**, according to the **eternal** purpose which He **purposed** in Christ Jesus our Lord

- Ephesians 3:10-11

...I write so that you may know how you ought to **conduct** yourself in the **house** of God, which is the **church** of the living **God**, the **pillar** and ground of the **truth**.

- 1 Timothy 3:15

of the _____ _____ shall be established" (Isaiah 2:2). What is the Lord's house (1 Timothy 3:15)? _____

When would the Lord's house be established?

_____

_____

Show that the time period in Acts 2, when the church is first spoken of as being in existence (verse 47), is "in the last days" (verses 16-17). _____

_____

_____

The church originated among all nations

The prophecy of Isaiah continues, "And _____ _____ shall flow to it" (Isaiah 2:2). Who was present on the day of Pentecost as recorded in Acts two (verse 5)? _____

_____

The church originated in Jerusalem

Isaiah's prophecy states:

Many people shall come and say,
"Come, and let us go up to the
_____ of the _____,
To the house of the God of Jacob;
He will teach us His ways,
And we shall walk in His paths."
For out of _____ shall go forth the law,
And the word of the Lord from
_____ (Isaiah 2:3).

What is "the mountain of the Lord" (Zechariah 8:3)?

_____

Where did the Lord say His house would be built (Zechariah 1:16)? _____

_____

Where would the foundation be laid (Isaiah 28:16)?

_____

Observe where the church began in Acts 2:5.

_____

The church originated in the days of the Roman kings

Read and study Daniel 2. King Nebuchadnezzar of Babylon has a dream and God through Daniel reveals the king's dream and the interpretation.

1. Tell what each of the following represent:

    a. Head of gold _____

    _____

    b. Breast and arms of silver _____

    _____

    c. Belly and thighs of brass _____

    _____

    d. Legs and feet of iron_____

    _____

2. Daniel 2:44 records, "And in the days of these kings the God of heaven will set up a _____ which shall never be destroyed; and the kingdom shall not be left to other people; it shall break in pieces and consume all these, and it shall stand forever." To what does "the days of these kings" refer? _____

    _____

    What would God do "in the days of these kings"? _____

    _____

    What is the kingdom of God (Matthew 16:18-19; Colossians 1:13, 24; Hebrews 12:23, 28)? ____

    _____

    The kingdom was "_____ _____" in the

...The time is **fulfilled**, and the **kingdom** of God is **at hand**. Repent, and believe in the **gospel**.

- Mark 1:15

days of John and Jesus (Matthew 3:1-2; 4:17). Jesus came into Galilee preaching, "The time is _____, and the kingdom of God is _____ _____" (Mark 1:15). Show that the kingdom, the church, came into existence "in the days of these kings" as prophesied by Daniel._____

_____

_____

The church originated when the Son of Man came to the Ancient of Days

Daniel 7:13-14 records:

I was watching in the night visions,
And behold, One like the Son of Man,
Coming with the _____ of heaven!
He _____ the Ancient of Days,
And they brought him near before Him,
Then to Him was given dominion and glory
and a _____.

When did this take place (Acts 1:9-11)? _____
_____

The church originated in the lifetime of some disciples

The Lord said, "Assuredly, I say to you that there are some standing here who will not taste _____ till they see the _____ of God present" (Mark 9:1). Either the kingdom, the church, originated in their lifetime and Jesus was wrong about it, or there are people about 2,000 years old roaming the earth today who are still waiting for the kingdom of God to come! Which of these do you believe is correct?_____

_____

...Assuredly, I say to you that there are **some** standing here who will not taste **death** till they see the **kingdom** of God present with **power**.

- Mark 9:1

The church originated after the Holy Spirit came

The Lord told His disciples that some of them would see "the kingdom of God present with _____" (Mark 9:1). If we can identify when the power came, we will discover when the church came into existence. According to Acts 1:8, when would power be given to the apostles? _____

When did this occur (Acts 2:4)? _____

The church originated when the seed of the kingdom was planted

The Parable of the Sower is about (Matthew 13:1-23; Mark 4:1-20; Luke 8:1-18):

What is the seed? _____

When was the seed of the kingdom first planted among all nations (Luke 24:47; Acts 2)? _____

What principle concerning seed was established in the beginning (Genesis 1:11-12)?_____
If seed is preserved properly and planted in good soil, what will it produce?

The one true church originated in Jerusalem, on the first Pentecost following the resurrection and ascension of Jesus Christ, when the word of God was first preached among all nations, about AD 33. Understanding the origin of the church will help us distinguish the one true church built by Christ from "churches" of modern, human origin.

Some questions from our study

1. Take your Bible and show the following:

    The church did not originate before the foundation of the world, in the garden of Eden, or in the days of Abraham. _____

The church did not originate prior to the days of John and Jesus.

_____

_____

_____

The church did not originate during the days of John the Baptist.

_____

_____

_____

The church did not originate before the Lord's death, resurrection, or ascension. _____

_____

_____

Beginning in Acts 2, we read of "the church" and of those who were in the kingdom. _____

_____

_____

2. What are some things which must be true *IF* the church originated *BEFORE* Acts 2? _____

_____

_____

_____

Name of the One True Church

A name "is a word or a combination of words by which a person, place, or thing, a body or class, or any object of thought is designated, called, or known." This study takes a look at the word or words by which the one true church is designated, called, or known.

What's in a name?

Some seem to think that it really doesn't make any difference what name one wears religiously; there's nothing in a name. The Scriptures teach that a name is of great significance.

1. God changed the names of some people.
   Abram: "No longer shall your name be called Abram, but your _____ shall be _____" (Genesis 17:5).
   Sarai: "Then God said to Abraham, 'As for Sarai your wife, you shall not call her name Sarai, but _____ shall be her _____'" (Genesis 17:15).
   Jacob: "And He said, 'Your name shall no longer be called Jacob, but _____" (Genesis 32:28). Also Genesis 35:10.

2. The Bible talks about a good name. The wise man said, "A _____ _____ is to be chosen rather than great riches" (Proverbs 22:1). "A _____ _____ is better than precious ointment" (Ecclesiastes 7:1).

3. If there's nothing in a name, would you name your son Ahab or your daughter Jezebel? Why

> ## Memory Verse
>
> ...the **churches of Christ** greet you.
>
> - Romans 16:16

are men sent to prison for signing the wrong name to a check? Have your employer make out your paychecks with my name on them instead of yours.

4.   Salvation is in a name. "Nor is there _____ in any other, for there is no other _____ under heaven given among men, by which we must be saved" (Acts 4:12).

A new name

Isaiah prophesied concerning a new name to be given. Three passages predict this new name:

1.   Isaiah 56:5, "Even to them I will give in My house and within My walls a plan and a _____ better than that of sons and daughters; I will give them an everlasting name that shall not be cut off."

2.   Isaiah 62:2, "The Gentiles shall see your righteousness, and all kings your glory. You shall be called by a new _____, which the mouth of the Lord will name."

3.   Isaiah 65:15, "You shall leave your name as a curse to My chosen; for the Lord God will slay you, and call His servants by another _____."

4.   From these passages, what do you learn about the prophesied name? _____ _____ _____

...And the **disciples** were first called **Christians** in Antioch.

- Acts 11:26

As there are three passages in the Old Testament which predict the name, there are three passages in the New Testament which reveal the name:

1.   Acts 11:26, "And the disciples were first called _____ in Antioch."

2. Acts 26:28, "Then Agrippa said to Paul, 'You almost persuade me to become a
    _____.'"

3. 1 Peter 4:16, "Yet if anyone suffers as a
    _____, let him not be ashamed, but let him glorify God in this matter."

How the church is designed

The New Testament church really does not have an exclusive name, but is spoken of several different ways. Read the following passages and take note of the word or words by which the church is known:

1. Acts 2:47 _____

2. Acts 8:1 _____

3. Acts 20:28 _____

4. Romans 16:1 _____

5. 1 Corinthians 1:2 _____

6. Colossians 4:16 _____

7. 1 Thessalonians 1:1 _____

8. 1 Timothy 3:15 _____

9. Hebrews 12:23 _____

10. 1 Peter 5:13 _____

11. Revelation 2:1 _____

12. Revelation 2:8 _____

13. Romans 16:16 _____

14. 1 Corinthians 14:33 _____

15. 1 Corinthians 16:1 _____

16. Galatians 1:22_____

...And the Lord added to the **church** daily those who were being **saved**.

- Acts 2:47

Words by which members of the church are known

1. Acts 5:14 _____

2. Acts 6:1 _____

3. Acts 11:26 _____

4. Acts 9:32 _____

5. Colossians 1:2 _____

Principles concerning the name of the church

1. Wearing names of men is wrong (1 Corinthians 1:10-15).

2. Combine spiritual things with spiritual words. Paul penned, "Which things also we speak, not in words which man's wisdom teacheth, but which the Holy Spirit teacheth; combining spiritual things with spiritual words" (1 Corinthians 2:10-13, ASV).

3. Call Bible things by Bible names. "If any man speak, let him speak as the _____ of _____" (1 Peter 4:11).

The one true church is called by a name designated by God and found upon the pages of His Word. Is the name you wear religiously known to the Word of God? Can the name of the church to which you belong be found in the Bible?

Some questions from our study

1. How would you respond to one who suggests it really doesn't make any difference what name we wear religiously? _____
    _____
    _____

2. List the three passages which foretell a new name. _____
    _____
    _____

3. Where, in the New Testament, do you read of the name "Christian"?
    _____
    _____

4. What are some Scriptural designations of the one true church? _____

_____

_____

Worship of the One True Church

As we consider the one true church, we cast our attention to its worship. The way the Lord's church worships sets it apart from other religious groups. It serves as an identifying mark to those searching for the true church.

What is worship?

The American Heritage Dictionary defines worship as "ardent admiration or love," "adoration" and "to honor and love as a deity."

Vine's Expository Dictionary says it means "to make obeisance" or "do reverence to." In addition, it means "to revere" and "to honor religiously."

Biblically, the idea of worship falls into several different categories. Consider the following:

1. Glory of God. The Psalmist wrote, "_____ unto the LORD the _____ due to His name; _____ the LORD in the beauty of holiness" (Psalm 29:2). God is owed glory, and He is the recipient of it as He is worshipped.

2. Praise of God. David penned, "I will _____ You, O Lord my God, with all my heart, And I will _____ Your name forevermore" (Psalm 86:12). God is deserving of all the praise we can assemble, and it is offered to Him through worship.

3. Fear of God. Respecting God is part of man's duty. The wise man said, "Let us hear the

Memory Verse

God is **Spirit**, and those who **worship** Him must worship in **spirit** and **truth**.

- John 4:24

conclusion of the whole matter: _____ God and keep His commandments, For this is man's _____" (Ecclesiastess 12:13). Respect and reverence for God is presented to Him as He is worshipped.

Kinds of worship

Though most do not realize it, there are numerous kinds, or forms, of worship mentioned in the Bible.

1. Vain worship. In condemning the hypocrites, Jesus repeated Isaiah's prophecy saying, "And in _____ they _____ Me, Teaching as doctrines the commandments of men" (Matthew 15:9). Something which is vain is useless, or of no value.

   Worship can become vain in many different ways. Look up the following passages and note what invalidates worship.

   1) Matthew 6:1, 5 _____ _____

   2) Matthew 6:7 _____ _____

   3) Matthew 5:23-24 _____ _____

   4) Mark 7:7 _____ _____

2. Self-imposed worship. Paul wrote, "These things indeed have an appearance of wisdom in _____ religion, false humility, and neglect of the body, but are of no value against the indulgence of the flesh" (Colossians 2:23). This religion (or worship) is one based upon an individual's desire to please himself, and do

And when you **pray**, do not use **vain repetitions** as the **heathen** do. For they think that they will be **heard** for their **many words**.

- Matthew 6:7

what he pleases. This type of worship is often referred to as "will worship." These things are done with no regard to God or His Word and are simply not acceptable.

3. Truthful worship. "God is Spirit, and those who _____ Him must worship in spirit and _____" (John 4:24). Worshipping in truth merely means worshipping in the way and manner God has instructed. If God has specified how He desires His church to worship, then that is how it should be carried out.

4. Spirited worship. It is noticed in John 4:24, God also calls upon His church to not only worship in truth, but in "_____." This has to do with our attitude, or mind-set as God is worshipped.

Worship should be zealous and enthusiastic, and the minds of the worshippers should be completely in tune with what is being said and done.

Items of worship in the one true church

As one reads the New Testament and notes how the early church worshipped, he or she will notice the following actions.

1. Singing. The New Testament church was found to be singing, and was commanded to do such. The apostle commanded, "_____ to one another in psalms and hymns and spiritual songs, _____ and making melody in your heart to the Lord" (Ephesians 5:19).

   There are two kinds of music, vocal and mechanical. Under the Law of Moses, God's children were commanded to use mechanical instruments in their worship (2 Chronicles 29:35).

Speaking to one another in **psalms** and **hymns** and **spiritual** songs, **singing** and making **melody** in your **heart** to the Lord.

- Ephesians 5:19

We now are subject to the New Testament and are to follow its commands. Use the box below to help determine what God expects musically from the one true church.

Concordance Exercise	
Write the New Testament verse(s) which contain the words sung, sing or singing.	Write the New Testament verse(s) which instruct the church to play a mechanical instrument.

2. Praying. The early church was often found praying. The one true church should still be involved in such activity. Look up the following verses and make a note of who was praying, or for what the prayer was being offered.

    1) Acts 2:42 _____
    _____

    2) Acts 12:12 _____
    _____

    3) Acts 16:25 _____
    _____

    4) 1 Timothy 2:1 _____
    _____

3. Preaching and teaching. The knowledge gained through the teaching and preaching of God's Word is a bedrock of the one true church. Without faithful and able instruction from God's Word, the Lord's church would wither away.

    In the Great Commission, Jesus instructed, "Go therefore and make disciples of all the nations, baptizing them in the name of the Father and of the Son and of the Holy Spirit, _____ them to _____ all things that I have commanded you; and lo, I am with you always, even to the end of the age. Amen" (Matthew 28:19-20).

This is accomplished through the preaching of sermons (2 Timothy 4:2), but also through Bible studies of both public and private nature (Acts 20:20).

4. Lord's supper. Jesus instituted this prior to His death as recorded in Matthew 26:26-28. Paul reiterated these same sentiments in 1 Corinthians 11:23-26. Answer the following questions based upon your reading of these verses.

   1) What did Jesus say the bread was? _____
   _____

   2) What did Jesus identify the cup as? _____
   _____

   3) For what purpose was the blood of Jesus shed? _____
   _____

   4) Paul adds these actions should be done for what purpose? _____
   _____

This aspect of worship is to be carried out on the first day of the week. Luke wrote, "Now on the _____ day of the week, when the disciples came together to _____ bread, Paul, ready to depart the next day, spoke to them and continued his message until midnight" (Acts 20:7). This "breaking of bread" was the Lord's supper.

Since every week has a first day, then the one true church partakes of the Lord's supper every Sunday. For comparison, consider the

Now on the **first day** of the week, when the disciples came **together** to **break bread**...

- Acts 20:7

Old Testament command to remember the Sabbath day (Exodus 20:8). Which Sabbath day did the people of God keep? _____

_____

While partaking of the Lord's supper, the mind should be focused on the "Lord's _____" (1 Corinthians 11:29). The one true church needs this weekly reminder.

5. Giving. Also on the first day of the week, the one true church is called upon to "lay something _____" (1 Corinthians 16:2). Each individual determines to make a free-will offering. According to 2 Corinthians 9:7, what kind of giver does the Lord love? _____

_____

Consider the good example of the widow in Mark 12:42-43. In monetary terms, did she give more than the rich folks? _____

Did she give everything she had? _____

With whom was Jesus more impressed? _____

_____

Members of the one true church should realize the attitude with which the offering is given is as important as the amount given.

Worship brings wonderful blessings

Being consistent in worship and attendance will produce great benefits and blessings in your life. It will give you a peace which can be found in no other person or place. It will cause your heart to soar in ways and to places beyond your imagination. Be sure it does these things for you!

Some questions from our study

1. How would you define vain worship? _____

_____

_____

2. What does it mean to "worship in spirit?"_____

_____

_____

3. What two elements constitute the Lord's supper, and what do they represent? _____

   _____

   _____

4. With what attitude should one give on the first day of the week? _____

   _____

   _____

Work of the One True Church

Christ gave gifts to make the church sufficient, "for the equipping of the saints, for the work of ministry, for the edifying of the body of Christ" (Ephesians 4:7-16). This study explores what the Bible teaches concerning the work of the one true church.

The work is directed by Christ

1. Christ has all authority. "_____ _____ has been given to Me in heaven and on earth" (Matthew 28:18).

2. Christ is Head over the church. "And He put all things under His feet, and gave Him to be _____ over all things to the church, which is His body" (Ephesians 1:22-23).

3. The church is subject unto Christ. "Therefore, just as the church is _____ to Christ" (Ephesians 5:24).

4. All is to be done in the name of Christ. "And whatever you do in word or deed, do _____ in the _____ of the Lord Jesus" (Colossians 3:17). Explain what doing all in the name of Christ means (Acts 4:7). _____ _____ _____

The work is spiritual in nature

1. God, the divine architect of the church (Ephesians 3:10-11), is spiritual. "God is _____" (John 4:24).

Memory Verse

Therefore, my beloved brethren, be **steadfast**, immovable, always **abounding** in the **work** of the Lord, knowing that your **labor** is **not in vain** in the **Lord**.

- 1 Corinthians 15:58

2. The mission of the builder (Matthew 16:18) and purchaser (Acts 20:28) of the church was spiritual. "For the Son of Man has come to _____ and to _____ that which was _____" (Luke 19:10).

3. The church is spiritual. It is a spiritual house. "You also, as living stones, are being built up a _____ house, a holy priesthood, to offer up _____ sacrifices acceptable to God through Jesus Christ" (1 Peter 2:5). It is a kingdom not of this world. Jesus said, "My kingdom is not of _____ _____. If My kingdom were of this world, My servants would fight...but now My kingdom is not from here" (John 18:36). Paul penned, "For the kingdom of God is not _____ and _____, but righteousness and peace and joy in the Holy Spirit" (Romans 14:17).

The work is threefold in scope

1. Evangelism: Preaching the gospel. Ephesians 4:12 mentions "the _____ of the body of Christ." The Lord commissioned the apostles, "Go into all the world and _____ the _____ to every creature. He who believes and is baptized will be saved; but he who does not believe will be condemned" (Mark 16:15-16). What is God's saving power (Romans 1:16; 1 Corinthians 15:1-2)? _____ _____

    The church is "the _____ and _____ of the _____" (1 Timothy 3:15). It is said concerning the church of the Thessalonians, "For from you the word of the Lord has _____ _____" (1 Thessalonians 1:8). This work

For I am not ashamed of the **gospel** of Christ, for it is the **power** of God to **salvation** for everyone who **believes**, for the Jew first and also for the Greek.

- Romans 1:16

was done as disciples "went everywhere
_____ the word" (Acts 8:4) and as
local churches supported the preaching of the
gospel. Paul defended the right of men to be
supported by the church while they preach the
gospel (1 Corinthians 9:1-14). The local church
may send and support men as they preach
the gospel in other fields. Paul told the church
at Corinth, "I robbed other churches, taking
_____ from them, to minister to you"
(2 Corinthians 11:8). The church at Antioch sent
Paul, Barnabas, and others on evangelistic
trips which resulted in souls being saved and
churches being established (Acts 13-21). The
church at Philippi sent to Paul as he preached
the word in Thessalonica (Philippians 4:15-16).

2. Edification: Building up Christians. The Lord
   made provisions "For the _____ of
   the _____" (Ephesians 4:12). Verse
   16 records, "From whom the whole body, joined
   and knit together by what every joint supplies,
   according to the effective working by which
   every part does its share, causes growth of the
   body for the _____ of itself in love."
   What is the meaning of the word "edify"? ____

   _____

   The church is edified through the Word of God.
   Acts 20:32, "So now, brethren, I commend you
   to God and to the _____ of His grace,
   which is able to _____ you _____ and
   give you an inheritance among all those who
   are sanctified." Read 1 Corinthians 14:1-6. How
   does the church receive edifying? _____

   _____

3. Benevolence: Relieving needy saints. This is
   "the work of _____" (Ephesians 4:12).

> For the
> **equipping** of
> the **saints** for
> the work of
> **ministry**, for
> the **edifying**
> of the **body** of
> Christ.
>
> - Ephesians 4:12

> If any **believing** man or woman has **widows**, let them **relieve** them, and do not let the **church** be **burdened**, that it may relieve those who are **really** widows.
>
> - 1 Timothy 5:16

The church at Jerusalem engaged in benevolent work at home, among themselves (Acts 2:44-45; 4:32-35; 6:1-4). The church in Antioch sent relief to the brethren in Judea (Acts 11:27-30). The churches of Macedonia and Achaia raised a contribution for the poor saints in Jerusalem (Romans 15:25-27; 1 Corinthians 16:1-3; 2 Corinthians 8-9). This work of the church is limited even among needy saints as Paul told Timothy, "If any believing man or woman has widows, let them relieve them, and _____

_____ _____ _____ _____ _____ _____, that it may relieve those who are really widows" (1 Timothy 5:16).

The work is supported by its members

God's plan for raising funds to do this work involves each member, according to his ability, laying by him in store upon the first day of the week (1 Corinthians 16:1-2; 2 Corinthians 8:12). Can you think of some Scriptural principles that govern our giving? _____
_____
_____

By the way, this is the only Scriptural way the church has of raising money to do its work. If there's another way, please tell us what it is and provide the Scripture that authorizes it. _____
_____

If this is the only Scriptural way the church has of raising money, every other way of raising money is unauthorized. What are some other ways churches established by men have of raising money today?
_____
_____
_____

The individual and the church

It's been said that, since the church is made up of Christians, what the Christian does the church does, that if it is scriptural for the individual to do it, then it is scriptural for the church to do it, too. This is not true! The Scriptures make a distinction between what an individual may do and what the church as such may do. How do the following Scriptures distinguish between actions of an individual and the church?

Matthew 18:15-17 _____

_____

1 Timothy 5:16_____

_____

We must keep true to the mission the Lord has assigned to His church and not turn aside to every work thought good by men. Remember,

"For My thoughts are not your thoughts,
Nor are your ways My ways," says the Lord.
"For as the heavens are higher than the earth,
So are My ways higher than your ways,
And My thoughts than your thoughts" (Isaiah 55:8-9).

Some questions from our study

1. Who directs the work of the church? _____

   _____

2. Show that the work of the church is spiritual in nature. _____

   _____

3. What is the threefold work of the church? _____

   _____

4. How is the work of the church supported? _____

   _____

5. What are some differences between the individual and the church with respect to the work of the church? _____

   _____

   _____

Organization of the One True Church

One identifiable mark of the one true church is the way in which it is organized. It is in order. The organization of the local church comes as a result of reading and studying God's Word and putting it into action.

God and His Word have always called for order

The Lord's church needing to be organized, or ordered, is nothing new with God. He and His people have always been an organized group. At one time, God corrected His people because they did not "_____ Him about the proper _____" (1 Chronicles 15:13).

Look up the following verses and make a record of what was said to be or needed to be "in order."

1. Genesis 22:9 _____
   _____

2. 2 Kings 20:1; Isaiah 38:1 _____
   _____

3. Job 33:5 _____
   _____

4. Acts 11:4 _____
   _____

5. 1 Corinthians 11:34 _____
   _____

6. 1 Corinthians 14:40 _____
   _____

Memory Verse

Paul and Timothy, bondservants of Jesus Christ, To all the **saints** in Christ Jesus who are in Philippi, with the **bishops** and **deacons**.

- Philippians 1:1

For our **citizenship** is in **heaven**, from which we also eagerly wait for the **Savior**, the Lord Jesus Christ.

- Philippians 3:20

Organization and order are especially important when it comes to the governing of a local body of God's people. Titus was left in Crete for this very reason. To him Paul wrote, "For this reason I left you in Crete, that you should set in _____ the things that are lacking, and appoint _____ in every city as I commanded you" (Titus 1:5).

Organization of the Lord's church

There are no earthly headquarters of the one true church. There are no national or global gatherings of its leaders. Since Jesus is the "head of the church" (Ephesians 5:23), the headquarters of the church are in heaven since Jesus is there (Philippians 3:20).

Paul offers the perfect snapshot of how a local group of God's people is organized. He wrote, "Paul and Timothy, bondservants of Jesus Christ, To all the _____ in Christ Jesus who are in Philippi, with the _____ and _____" (Philippians 1:1). This is the local church in a nutshell...bishops (elders), deacons and saints.

Qualifications of elders

Each individual wishing to serve in the capacity of an elder must meet certain God-given qualifications. You can read about them in 1 Timothy 3:1-7 and Titus 1:6-9. We have divided these into three categories: positive, negative and family qualifications. Please consider the following brief explanations and also the supplied companion verse.

Positive qualifications

1.   Man. The one wanting to serve as an elder must be male. We know this not only because

of the word "man," but also by virtue the candidate is a husband (1 Timothy 3:1).

2. Desires the position. He has a proper longing for the office. This is not a desire for glory or fame, but a craving for fulfilling God's need for leaders (Matthew 6:1, 5).

3. Blameless. He is not "perfect," though many have made this qualification mean such. It describes a man who realizes he has sinned but has made things right with God and others (Daniel 6:4).

4. Temperate, or self-Controlled. He has superior control. Nothing masters him, he masters everything in his life. He exercises supreme constraint (1 Corinthians 9:25-27).

5. Sober-minded. He does not allow anything into his life which would dull his ability to be alert and aware. While this could have to do with alcohol, it should be noted many other things could dull a man's senses (1 Peter 5:8).

6. Of good behavior. He has a reputation of acting upright and moral. His ethics are beyond question (Proverbs 11:3).

7. Hospitable. He exhibits great care and concern for others, especially those who are guests and strangers. He is willing to help any who need it (1 Peter 4:9).

8. Able to teach. He has studied the Word of God in such a way that he can ably and effectively instruct others about their responsibility to God (2 Timothy 2:2).

9. Gentle. He deals with others, especially those of God's family, with kindness, patience and understanding (Ephesians 4:32).

> This is a faithful saying: If a **man** desires the position of a **bishop**, he desires a **good work**.
>
> - 1 Timothy 3:1

10. Has a good testimony of those who are outside. He carries with him a good reputation concerning those who are not members of the Lord's church (Philippians 4:8).

11. A lover of what is good. He exempts himself from evil dealings and evil company. He surrounds himself with those who are decent people (Proverbs 13:20).

12. Just. He is equitable and fair in his treatment and judgment of others. He does not utilize double standards in his assessments (Micah 6:8).

13. Holy. He is a man who exhibits great respect and reverence for God and His Word. His life stands out from those of the world (Romans 12:1-2).

14. Holding fast the faithful word. He refuses to deviate from the truth found in God's Word. He does not add to or detract from it (Revelation 22:18-19).

Negative qualifications

1. Not given to wine. He, in no way or in no amount, allows alcohol to play a role in his life. He understands the danger which it presents (Proverbs 23:29-35).

2. Not violent. He is able to regulate his emotions in such a way he is not tempted to physically lash out at others (Romans 12:18).

3. Not greedy for money. He withstands the lure of riches. He works honestly for a fair wage, and is satisfied (1 Timothy 6:6-10).

4. Not quarrelsome. He does not fight about everything. To him, not every fight is worth getting into. He knows the best thing, at times, is to remain quiet (1 Timothy 6:12).

If it is possible, as much as depends on you, **live peaceably** with all men.

- Romans 12:18

5. Not covetous. He does not see the possessions of others and have a desire for them. He is happy with God's blessings and gifts for him (Philippians 4:11-13).

6. Not a novice. He is not a new or recent convert. He has been a child of God long enough to have gained valuable experience in decision-making (1 Kings 12:6-15).

7. Not self-willed. He puts himself last quite frequently. He knows God comes first and others next. He is not selfish with his time, talent or treasure (Philippians 2:1-4).

8. Not quick-tempered. He is patient with his words and the ways in which he reacts. He maintains composure when others around him lose theirs (Luke 21:19).

Family qualifications

1. He is the husband of one wife. He is married at the time of his appointment. He sees and understands his wife's importance to his success (Genesis 2:18).

2. He rules his own house well. He has his finger on the pulse of the family. He lovingly and fervently guides his wife and children toward heaven (Ephesians 6:4).

3. He has faithful children. He is in possession of children who are faithful to their earthly father and their heavenly Father. He has children who have obeyed the gospel plan of salvation (2 John 4).

I **rejoiced** greatly that I have found some of your **children** walking in **truth**, as we received **commandment** from the Father.

- 2 John 4

Qualifications of deacons

Those who desire to be a deacon must also meet qualifications. They are not as stringent as those for an elder, yet it is important they are met. Read 1 Timothy 3:8-10, 12-13 and supply the qualifications in the space below.

_____

_____

_____

_____

Wives of elders and deacons

The Bible additionally offers information concerning the wives of elders and deacons. The apostle addresses this in 1 Timothy 3:11. Write below the characteristics needing to be found in these ladies.

_____

_____

_____

_____

The work of elders and deacons

Elders and deacons work together for the good of the local flock. Their respective works may be different, but they both are vital.

The elders' chief concern is the spiritual well-being of the flock. They are to "_____ the flock of God which is _____ you" (1 Peter 5:2). The elders are to ensure the flock's diet consists of wholesome, sound doctrine. Peter also reminded the elders they were to be "_____ to the flock" (1 Peter 5:3). Elders should be men of high spiritual caliber, and serve as good influences. Also, elders are to "take _____ ... to all the _____" (Acts 20:28). That is, the spiritual safety of the flock is paramount.

The deacons' work falls under the oversight of the elders. A reading of Acts 6:1-8 will serve as an excellent blueprint for the working relationship between elders and deacons. The elders spiritually care for the flock, and need men (deacons) to help care for the physical aspects of the church. For example, the building and grounds, the care of widows, the benevolent work, the class material, and the website, etc.

The need for local organization

There is absolute genius in God's plan for the organization in the local body of God's people. This is why Paul was appointing "_____ in every church" (Acts 14:23). A biblically organized body of believers, overseen by qualified elders and served by hard-working deacons, will see the joy of growth, unity and peace. May each local church be so fortunate to experience such!

Some questions from our study

1. For what specific reason was Titus left in Crete? _____

    _____

    _____

2. Where is the headquarters of the one true church, and why is it there?

    _____

    _____

3. Why would it be important for an elder not to be a novice, or new convert?_____

    _____

    _____

4. In your own words, explain the difference between the work of elders and the work of deacons. _____

    _____

    _____

Doctrine of the One True Church

The doctrine of the church is that which the church teaches. As Christ said, "My doctrine is not Mine, but His who sent Me" (John 7:16), the church of Christ has no doctrine of its own. The church simply continues in "the apostles' doctrine" (Acts 2:42), "the doctrine of Christ" (2 John 9).

Doctrine is teaching

The Scriptures clearly show that the doctrine of Christ refers to His teachings; His sayings; His Word.

Matthew 5:2: "Then He opened His mouth and _____ them, _____."

Matthew 7:28-29: "And so it was, when Jesus had ended these _____, that the people were astonished at His _____. for He _____ them as one having authority, and not as the scribes."

Mark 1:22: "And they were astonished at His _____, for He _____ them as one having authority, and not as the scribes."

Mark 4:1-2: "And He began to _____ by the sea. And a great multitude was gathered to Him, so that He got into a boat and sat on the sea; and the whole multitude was on the land facing the sea. Then He _____ them many things, by parables, and said to them in His _____."

Mark 12:35, 38: "Then Jesus answered and said, while He _____ in the temple...Then He said to them in His _____..."

Memory Verse

Whoever **transgresses** and does not **abide** in the **doctrine** of Christ **does not have** God. He who abides in the doctrine of Christ has both the **Father** and the **Son**.

- 2 John 9

Luke 4:31-32: "Then He went down to Capernaum, a city of Galilee, and was _____ them on the Sabbaths. And they were astonished at His _____, for His _____ was with authority."

John 18:19-20: "The high priest then asked Jesus about His disciples and His _____. Jesus answered him, 'I _____ openly to the world. I always _____ in synagogues and in the temple, where the Jews always meet, and in secret I have _____ nothing."

Acts 5:28: "'Did we not strictly command you not to _____ in this name? And look, you have filled Jerusalem with your _____.'"

Read Acts 13:6-12 and make a list of words and phrases that equate. _____
_____
_____

To extend the perimeters of fellowship, some try to limit the doctrine of Christ to teaching *about* Christ. This is a fallacy!

Admonitions and warnings concerning doctrine

Then Jesus said to them, "Take **heed** and **beware** of the **leaven** of the Pharisees and the Sadducees."

- Matthew 16:6

1. The Lord warned His disciples, "_____ _____ and _____ of the _____ of the Pharisees and the Sadducees" (Matthew 16:6). To what did the Lord refer? _____
_____
What about "a little leaven" (Galatians 5:9)?
_____

2. The Scriptures place emphasis on "_____ doctrine" (1 Timothy 1:10; 2 Timothy 4:3; Titus 1:9; 2:1). What does the

word "sound," as used in these verses, mean?

_____

_____

Would this imply that there is such a thing as doctrine or teaching that is not sound? _____

3. Christians must have their feet on the ground when it comes to doctrine. "As you therefore have received Christ Jesus the Lord, so walk in Him, _____ and _____ up in Him and _____ in the faith, as you have been taught, abounding in it with thanksgiving. _____ lest anyone cheat you through _____ and empty _____, according to the _____ of _____, according to the basic principles of the world, and not according to Christ" (Colossians 2:6-8). "That we should _____ _____ _____ _____, tossed to and fro and carried about with every _____ of _____, by the trickery of men, in the cunning craftiness of deceitful plotting" (Ephesians 4:14). Write out the exhortation of 1 Thessalonians 5:21. _____

_____

_____

Give the Bible "do not" of Hebrews 13:9. _____

_____

"Beloved, do not believe every spirit, but _____ the spirits, whether they are of God; because many false prophets have gone out into the world" (1 John 4:1). "You therefore, beloved, since you know this beforehand, _____ lest you also fall from your own steadfastness, being _____ _____ with the _____ of the wicked" (2 Peter 3:17).

Test all things; **hold fast** what is good.

- 1 Thessalonians 5:21

> **Take heed** to yourself and to the **doctrine**. **Continue** in them, for in doing this you will **save** both yourself and those who **hear** you.
>
> - 1 Timothy 4:16

4. Doctrine is connected with our salvation and fellowship with God. Paul wrote the Romans, "But God be thanked that though you were slaves of sin, yet you obeyed from the heart that _____ _____ _____ to which you were delivered. And having been set _____ _____ _____, you became slaves of righteousness" (Romans 6:17-18). Write out and memorize 1 Timothy 4:16:

    _____
    _____
    _____
    _____

    Read 2 John 9. Now draw a circle and allow that circle to represent the doctrine of Christ.

    Where must we be to have "both the Father and the Son"? _____
    Doctrine is also for our _____
    (1 Corinthians 14:6, 26).

5. We must be uncompromising toward error and false teachers. Discuss Paul's marvel (Galatians 1:6-9). _____

    _____
    _____

    Galatians 2:4-5: "And this occurred because of false brethren secretly brought in (who came in by stealth to spy out our liberty which we have in Christ Jesus, that they might bring us into bondage), to whom _____ _____

    _____ _____ _____

even for _____ _____." Why didn't they
yield or compromise? _____
_____
_____

What instruction did Paul give to the saints at
Rome in Romans 16:17-18? _____
_____
_____

The first responsibility of every gospel
preacher is to "_____ some that
they _____ _____ _____
_____" (1 Timothy 1:3).
From 1 Timothy 6:3-5, tell what we should do "If
anyone teaches otherwise." _____
_____
_____

6. What about "a divisive man" (Titus 3:10-11)?
    _____
    _____

"If anyone comes to you and does not
bring not this doctrine, _____ _____
_____ him into your house
nor greet him; for he who greets him shares
in his evil deeds" (2 John 10-11). What did the
Lord have against the church at Pergamos
(Revelation 2:14-15)?_____
_____
_____

> **Reject** a **divisive** man after the first and second **admonition**, knowing that such a person is **warped** and **sinning**, being **self-condemned**.
>
> - Titus 3:10-11

The Holy Scriptures are the sole and sufficient doctrine of the church

2 Timothy 3:15-17: "and that from childhood
you have known _____ _____
_____, which are able to make you
_____ _____ _____
through faith which is in Christ Jesus. All

_____ is given by inspiration of God, and is _____ _____ _____, for reproof, for correction, for instruction in righteousness, that the man of God may be complete, thoroughly equipped for every good work." Why the Scriptures and the Scriptures alone?

1. _____ is completely revealed therein (Romans 1:16-17).

2. Thoroughly equips for _____ (2 Timothy 3:17).

3. Contains _____ (John 16:13).

4. Furnishes unto _____ that pertain to _____ and _____ (2 Peter 1:3-4).

5. The faith _____ delivered unto the saints (Jude 3).

6. There is _____ faith (Ephesians 4:5).

7. "...that you all speak the _____ _____" (1 Corinthians 1:10).

The Scriptures are not to be added to, subtracted from, or amended in any way (Deuteronomy 4:2; 12:32; Proverbs 30:6; 1 Corinthians 4:6; Galatians 1:6-9; Revelation 22:18-19).

Objections to doctrines of men

Be prepared to discuss each of these:

1. They are made by men. _____ _____

2. They do not meet the needs of man. _____ _____

3. They must continually be revised. _____ _____

4. There is no authority behind them. _____ _____

5. They disagree and conflict with each other. _____ _____

6. They conflict with the Word of God. _____ _____

7.   They render our worship vain (Matthew 15:9). _____

_____

Testing the church by what it teaches

As "a tree is known by its fruit" (Matthew 12:33), the identity of any church may be clearly shown by testing its teachings by the Scriptures. Give some examples: _____

_____

_____

What about remaining with a group where error and false doctrine are taught? _____

_____

May it be said of us, "they continued steadfastly in the apostles' doctrine" (Acts 2:42). Apostasy comes when men "will not endure sound doctrine" (2 Timothy 4:2-4).

Some questions from our study

1.   Show from the Scriptures that the doctrine of Christ is things Christ teaches and not the things said about Christ. _____

_____

_____

_____

2.   Sound doctrine has a distinct ring to it. Read 1 Corinthians 14:7-8. Can you think of some "uncertain sound" trumpeted from pulpits today?

_____

_____

_____

_____

3.   What is the sole and sufficient doctrine of the church? _____

_____

_____

Give two reasons why this is so. _____

_____

_____

4.   Give three objections to the doctrines of men. _____

_____

_____

_____

Membership in the One True Church

The Scriptures often speak of membership in the church (Romans 12:4-5; 1 Corinthians 12:12-27; Ephesians 5:30). This lesson tells us *how* to become a member in the church of our Lord and what membership in the one true church *means*.

The glory and grandeur of the church

The church is far greater than all human institutions.

1. God is its author (Hebrews 3:4). It is "the _____ of God" (1 Corinthians 3:16). It is "a _____ _____ of God" (Ephesians 2:19-22). It is "the _____ of God" (1 Corinthians 1:2).

2. Christ is its Savior and Head. He "_____ _____ for her" (Ephesians 5:25). He is "the _____ of the body" (Ephesians 5:23). With His own blood He hath "_____" it (Acts 20:28). He is "the _____ over all things" (Ephesians 1:22).

3. All spiritual blessings are contained therein. The church is "the _____ of Him who fills all in all" (Ephesians 1:23). What does this mean? _____

   _____
   _____
   _____

   All spiritual blessings are "_____ _____" (Ephesians 1:3).

Memory Verse

Now you are the **body** of Christ, and **members** individually.

- 1 Corinthians 12:27

List some of God's spiritual blessings. _____

_____
_____
_____
_____

It is in the church that we enjoy every spiritual blessing God has provided for us in Christ Jesus. Christ's body and the church are one (Ephesians 1:22-23; Colossians 1:18). Christ and the church are inseparably connected (Ephesians 5:28-32). We are reconciled unto God in the body of Christ, which is the church (Ephesians 2:16; Colossians 1:18-20). We get into Christ and the church upon the same conditions and by the same process (Galatians 3:26-27; 1 Corinthians 12:13).

Entrance into the church

1. Christ regulates entrance. The church was built by Christ, wears His name, and is under His authority (Matthew 16:18; Romans 16:16; Matthew 28:18). He alone has the right to stipulate the rules of admission into the church. We have no right to change the rules of admission into the church (Deuteronomy 4:2; Galatians 1:6-9; 2 John 9-11).

2. Jesus speaks of kingdom entrance in the gospel accounts. Entrance is by a *spiritual birth*. "Unless one is _____ of _____ and the _____, he cannot _____ the _____ of God" (John 3:5). This birth requires three things: a person, water, and the Spirit. Entrance is by *conversion*. "Unless you are _____ and become as little children, you will by no means _____ the _____ of heaven" (Matthew 18:3).

> Jesus answered, "Most assuredly, I say to you, unless one is **born** of **water** and the **Spirit**, he cannot **enter** the **kingdom** of God.
>
> - John 3:5

Explain what it means to be converted. _____

_____

_____

Entrance is by *doing the Father's will.* "Not everyone who says to Me, 'Lord, Lord,' shall _____ the _____ of heaven; but he who _____ the _____ of My _____ in heaven" (Matthew 7:21). Using the Lord's statements in these passages, make a diagram showing how men enter the church.

3. Examples of entrance in the book of Acts. Remission of sins and entrance into the church go together. What folks in New Testament days did to receive the remission of sins they did to become members of the church (Acts 2:38, 41, 47). Every conversion in the book of Acts is a repetition of this same story. The conversion of the Jews on Pentecost (Acts 2), the Samaritans (Acts 8:5-12), Simon (Acts 8:13), the Ethiopian treasurer (Acts 8:26-39), Saul of Tarsus (Acts 9, 22, 26), Cornelius (Acts 10-11), Lydia (Acts 16:11-15), the Philippian jailer (Acts 16:25-34), the Corinthians (Acts 18:1-8) and the Ephesians (Acts 19:1-5) reveal folks entering the kingdom through hearing the word of God, believing it with all their heart, repenting of their sins, confessing their faith in Jesus as the Son of God and being baptized for the remission of sins.

Then Simon himself also **believed**; and when he was **baptized** he continued with Philip...

- Acts 8:13

What membership means

1. To be a citizen in the kingdom of Christ. Colossians 1:12-13 says, "giving thanks to the Father who has qualified us to be partakers of the inheritance of the saints in light. He has delivered us from the power of darkness and conveyed us _____ _____ _____ of the Son of His love."

2. To be a member of the body of which Christ is Savior and Head. "For as the body is one and has many members, but all the members of that one body, being many, are one body, so also is Christ. For by one Spirit we were all baptized _____ _____ _____— whether Jews or Greeks, whether slaves or free—and have all been made to drink into one Spirit" (1 Corinthians 12:12-13).

> You also, as **living stones**, are being built up a **spiritual** house, a holy **priesthood**, to offer up spiritual **sacrifices** acceptable to God through Jesus Christ.
>
> - 1 Peter 2:5

3. To be a child in God's family. "For you are all _____ _____ _____ through faith in Christ Jesus. For as many of you as were _____ _____ _____ have put on Christ" (Galatians 3:26-27).

4. To be a stone in the temple of God. "you also, _____ _____ _____, are being built up a spiritual house, a holy priesthood, to offer up spiritual sacrifices acceptable to God through Jesus Christ" (1 Peter 2:5).

5. To be married to Christ. "Therefore, my brethren, you also have become dead to the law through the body of Christ, that you may _____ _____ to _____—even to Him who was raised from the dead, that we should bear fruit to God" (Romans 7:4).

6. To be a sheep in the flock of God. "Therefore take heed to yourselves
    and to all _____ _____, among which the Holy Spirit
    has made you overseers, to shepherd the church of God which He
    purchased with His own blood" (Acts 20:28).

7. To be a worker in the Lord's vineyard. "For the kingdom of heaven
    is like a landowner who went out early in the morning to hire
    _____ _____ _____ _____" (Matthew 20:1).

Local church membership

The word "church" is used in two senses: *Universal*—includes every saved
person on earth (Acts 2:47). *Local*—designates the saved gathered together
in a particular location (1 Corinthians 1:2).

Since the local church is the only unit of organization known in the New
Testament for carrying forward the work of the church, a Christian must
be part of a local church. There is no such thing in the Scriptures as
"membership at large" in the church of Christ.

Paul, an example (Acts 9:26-30; 11:22-30; 13:1-3; 14:25-28). _____
_____
_____

The example of Apollos (Acts 18:24-28). _____
_____
_____

Responsibilities of local church membership. Every relationship in life that
is worthwhile involves responsibility. Membership in the church brings the
highest and holiest privileges, and with those blessings come the greatest
of responsibilities. List some of these obligations: _____
_____
_____

We make a plea to those outside of Christ to accept the terms of entrance
into the church set forth by Christ in the New Testament and be "added
to the church" by the Lord (Acts 2:47). Salvation is in the body of Christ
(Ephesians 5:23). As Saul "tried to join the disciples" at Jerusalem, we
encourage you to join yourself to the disciples here and carry out your
responsibilities in the local church.

Some questions from our study

1. Show that the church is the greatest of all institutions. _____

    _____

    _____

2. Explain how one becomes a member of the church. _____

    _____

    _____

3. What does it mean to be a member of the one true church? _____

    _____

    _____

4. What are some responsibilities one has a member of the local church?

    _____

    _____

    _____

    _____

Importance of the One True Church

It is impossible to overstate the importance of the one true church. It is very important, and those who study the Bible understand this to be so. A thorough understanding of the importance of the Lord's church will cause one to love and cherish it.

Some have tried to diminish its importance

Over the centuries, some have downplayed the importance of the one true church. This false idea teaches Jesus was unable to set up His kingdom and had to "settle" for the church as a temporary solution, a band-aid of sort. This diminishes the importance of it!

This confusion comes as a result of not understanding that the "kingdom" is the "church." When one reads Matthew 16:18-19, notice the words "church" and "kingdom" are, most of the time, interchangeable. When the church was born, so was the kingdom.

Look up the following verses and make a note of what is said regarding the kingdom, or the church.

1. Colossians 1:13 _____
   _____

2. Colossians 4:11 _____
   _____

3. Revelation 1:9 _____
   _____

Memory Verse

Therefore take heed to **yourselves** and to all the **flock**, among which the Holy Spirit has made you **overseers**, to **shepherd** the **church** of God which He **purchased** with His own **blood**.

- Acts 20:28

It becomes evident then, there were those living in Bible days that belonged to the *kingdom*. This meant they belonged to the *church*. Let us strive to comprehend and appreciate the importance of the one true church.

Its importance can be seen in its planning

The one true church was not merely an afterthought of God or a bandage to cover up an unforeseen problem. In fact, it was just the opposite.

Paul penned, "to the intent that now the manifold wisdom of God might be made known by the _____ to the principalities and powers in the heavenly places, according to the _____ purpose which He accomplished in Christ Jesus our Lord" (Ephesians 3:10-11).

The church is so important, it was in the mind of God before He even began to create the world. Anything planned in this fashion must be of great and significant importance!

Its importance can be seen in its purchase price

The one true church was purchased, and the price of it was very steep. In speaking to the Ephesian elders, Paul makes us aware of the price.

"Therefore take heed to yourselves and to all the flock, among which the Holy Spirit has made you overseers, to shepherd the _____ of God which He _____ with His own _____" (Acts 20:28).

Jesus was called by His Father to leave Heaven (Philippians 2:5-8), come to earth, offer Himself and

> So Christ was **offered** once to bear the sins of **many**. To those who **eagerly wait** for Him He will appear a **second** time, apart from sin, for **salvation**.
>
> - Hebrews 9:28

"bear the _____ of _____" (Hebrews 9:28). Please take time to investigate the following verses, and in the afforded space, write down what happened to Jesus as He was offering His life.

1. Matthew 26:36-44 _____
   _____

2. Matthew 26:47-50 _____
   _____

3. Matthew 26:69-75 _____
   _____

4. Matthew 27:26 _____
   _____

5. Matthew 27:28 _____
   _____

6. Matthew 27:29 _____
   _____

7. Matthew 27:30 _____
   _____

8. Matthew 27:31 _____
   _____

9. Matthew 27:35 _____
   _____

The purchase price of the one true church was Jesus, His body and His blood. Anything costing this much must be of immense importance!

Its importance can be seen in its value

The Bible places great value upon the one true church. Jesus presented two short parables to illustrate this. Read Matthew 13:44-46, and answer the following questions.

Again, the **kingdom** of heaven is like **treasure** hidden in a field, which a man found and hid; and for **joy** over it he goes and **sells all** that he has and **buys** that field.

- Matthew 13:44

1. The kingdom is compared to what in verse 44?

   _____

   _____

2. How much did the man sell in order to purchase this great find? _____

   _____

3. What did the merchant man find in verse 46?

   _____

   _____

4. What did he sell in order to buy this precious item? _____

   _____

The one true church is so enormously valuable. Any institution with this much worth placed upon it is of enormous importance!

Its importance can be seen in its population

...And the **Lord** added to the **church** daily those who were being **saved**.

- Acts 2:47

Some of the best people on God's beautiful earth are His people, the people of God. It is a family unlike any other. This great family had its beginning on the day of Pentecost, when the "_____ to the _____ daily those who were being _____" (Acts 2:47).

This family (Ephesians 3:15) shares a wonderful love with each other which can be found in no other place or organization. It is necessary for spiritual survival to have this kind of family who cares for each other.

This is the family which will "_____ with those who rejoice, and _____ with those who weep" (Romans 12:15).

This is the family in which every member is "_____"
(1 Corinthians 12:22). As well, when one member "_____, all
the members suffer with it," and if one member is "_____, all
the members rejoice with it" (1 Corinthians 12:26).

All Christians need help in gaining a home in Heaven, and a loving,
forgiving family meets this need. Any group providing this need is of great
importance!

Its importance can be seen in its destiny

One of the many great things about the one true church is its destiny. It
truly is out of this world. While the church serves as the "_____
and _____ of the truth" (1 Timothy 3:15) now, its future and final
destination is an eternal home with God.

This is what Paul had in mind when writing, "Then comes the end, when He
delivers the _____ to _____ the Father, when He puts an
end to all rule and all authority and power" (1 Corinthians 15:24).

Since the church is where God places the saved (Acts 2:47), and the saved
will formulate the population of Heaven (Revelation 21:24), then being part
of the one true church is tremendously important!

The one true church

There has never been or ever will be an institution more important than
the one true church. No other family on earth surpasses the family it
represents in significance or impact. May each individual see this to be true!

Some questions from our study

1. What passage helps us to appreciate the *church* and *kingdom* are
   usually interchangeable terms? _____
   _____
   _____

2. When did God start planning the one true church? _____
   _____
   _____

3. What several things did Jesus endure in order to be the purchase price
    of the church? _____

    _____

    _____

    _____

    _____

4. State in your own words how valuable the family of God can be in
    achieving a home in Heaven. _____

    _____

    _____

    _____

    _____

General Characteristics of the One True Church

When a child goes missing, there is a missing persons report in which are detailed the characteristics of that person. When one locates the individual who possesses all those characteristics, then by identification they have found the person. This is how it works with the one true church. When we learn the general characteristics of the church, we can then distinguish it from all others.

It was built by Christ and purchased with His own blood

It was built by Christ. Jesus announced, "And I say also to you that you are Peter, and on this rock I will _____ _____ _____, and the gates of Hades shall not prevail against it" (Matthew 16:18).

It was purchased with the blood of Christ. Paul charged the elders of the church at Ephesus, "Therefore take heed to yourselves and to all the flock, among which the Holy Spirit has made you overseers, to shepherd the _____ of God which He _____ with His own _____" (Acts 20:28).

It is, therefore, a divine institution.

It was established in Jerusalem with Christ as its foundation

It was established in Jerusalem. It was prophesied,

Memory Verse

There is **one body**...

- Ephesians 4:4

Now it shall come to pass in the latter days
That the mountain of the Lord's house
Shall be established on the top of the mountains,
And shall be exalted above the hills;
And all nations shall flow to it.
Many people shall come and say,
"Come, and let us go up to the mountain of the Lord,
To the house of the God of Jacob;
He will teach us His ways,
And we shall walk in His paths."
For out of Zion shall go forth the law,
And the word of the Lord from Jerusalem (Isaiah 2:2-3).

Show, from Acts chapter 2, that the church was established in Jerusalem, as prophesied by Isaiah.

_____
_____
_____

...**Repentance** and **remission of sins** should be **preached** in His name to all nations, **beginning at Jerusalem**.

- Luke 24:47

Both the Lord and Peter pointed to Jerusalem as the "beginning" (Luke 24:47; Acts 11:15).

It had Christ as its foundation. "For no other _____ can anyone lay than that which is laid, which is _____ _____" (1 Corinthians 3:11). It was "built on the _____ of the apostles and prophets, _____ _____ Himself being the _____ _____"
(Ephesians 2:20).

It had divinely appointed names by which it and its members were known

It was prophesied in the Old Testament that the Lord would call His people by a _____ name (Isaiah 56:5; 62:2; 65:15). As there are three passages in the Old Testament that foretell the name, there are three passages in the New

Testament that reveal the name—Acts 11:26; 26:28; 1 Peter 4:16. The name that the Lord's people wear individually is the name _____.

Now, read the following passages and take note of how the church is spoken of.

Romans 16:16 _____
_____

1 Corinthians 1:2 _____
_____

Hebrews 12:23 _____
_____

Remember, the church is a spiritual house (1 Peter 2:5), and we are to combine spiritual words with spiritual things (1 Corinthians 2:13).

It was governed wholly by divine authority

Christ claimed, "All _____ has been given to Me in heaven and on earth" (Matthew 28:18). If Christ has all authority, how much does that leave for anyone else? _____
Where did God the Father set His Son Jesus (Ephesians 1:21-23)? _____
_____

The bride figure of the church expresses this concept well—"For the husband is the head of the wife, as also Christ is _____ of the church; and He is the Savior of the body. Therefore, just as the church is _____ to Christ, so let the wives be to their own husbands in everything" (Ephesians 5:23-24). Do the Scriptures ever make mention of human conferences, conventions, councils, or synods?_____

And Jesus came and spoke to them, saying, "All **authority** has been given to **Me** in **heaven** and on **earth**.

- Matthew 28:18

It had a simple, local, and independent form of government

Elders (also called bishops and pastors) were appointed in every church in every city to feed and lead the local congregation. "So when they had appointed elders in every church" (Acts 14:23). Why did Paul leave Titus in Crete (Titus 1:5)? _____

_____

_____

The elders in the church at Ephesus were instructed, "Therefore take heed to yourselves and to all the flock, among which the Holy Spirit has made you _____, to _____ the church of God which He purchased with his own blood" (Acts 20:28). Thus, elders, bishops (overseers) and pastors (shepherds) all refer to one and the same office. There was not a plurality of churches under one bishop, but a plurality of bishops in one church. Paul began his letter to the church in Philippi with the words, "To all the _____ in Christ Jesus who are in Philippi, with the _____ and _____" (Philippians 1:1). What exhortation did Peter give to elders (1 Peter 5:1-4)? _____

_____

_____

It had specific conditions of membership

The Lord commissioned the apostles to preach faith, repentance and baptism as conditions of salvation (Matthew 28:19; Mark 16:15-16; Luke 24:46-47). This commission was first executed on the first Pentecost following the resurrection and ascension of Jesus. Read Acts 2 to find out how folks became members of the church when it was

Go therefore and make **disciples** of all the nations, **baptizing** them in the name of the **Father** and of the **Son** and of the **Holy Spirit**.

- Matthew 28:19

first established. _____
_____
_____

The rest of the book of Acts is a repetition of this story as folks heard the word of God, believed it, repented of their sins, confessed their faith in Jesus as the Son of God and were baptized for the remission of their sins. Paul wrote the Corinthians, "For by one Spirit we were all _____ into one body" (1 Corinthians 12:13). Remember the "one body" (Ephesians 4:4) "is the church" (Colossians 1:24).

> For by **one Spirit** we were all **baptized** into one **body**...
>
> - 1 Corinthians 12:13

It had a definite pattern of worship

Worship must be directed to God in spirit and in truth to be acceptable in His sight (John 4:24). Acts 2:42 records of the first church, "And they continued steadfastly in the apostles' _____ and _____, in the _____ _____ _____, and in _____." Ephesians 5:19 says, "speaking to one another in psalms and hymns and spiritual songs, _____ and making melody in your heart to the Lord." The Corinthians were taught, "On the _____ day of the week let each of you _____ something aside, storing up as he may prosper, that there be no collections when I come" (1 Corinthians 16:2). The worship of the early church was simple. They sang, prayed, taught the word of God, ate the Lord's supper, and gave of their means.

Penitent, faith-confessing believers were the subjects of baptism

Jesus said, "He who _____ and is baptized will be saved; but he who does not believe

> Therefore we were **buried** with Him through **baptism** into **death**, that just as Christ was **raised** from the **dead** by the glory of the Father, even so we also should walk in **newness of life**.
>
> - Romans 6:4

will be condemned" (Mark 16:16). When asked, "What shall we do?" (Acts 2:37), Peter answered, "_____, and let every one of you be baptized in the name of Jesus Christ for the remission of sins" (Acts 2:38). Prior to being baptized, what did the Ethiopian confess (Acts 8:37)? _____

_____

This is the bedrock truth upon which the church of Christ is built (Matthew 16:18)!

The action of baptism was immersion in water

The example of the traveling treasurer demonstrates this to be the case. Notice what took place in Acts 8:36-38. They _____ _____ some water, went _____ _____ the water, the baptism took place, and they _____ _____ _____ _____ the water. Paul addressed the Romans, "We were _____ with Him through baptism into death" (Romans 6:4). The only meaning of the word "baptism" in the first century was immersion. There were other words for sprinkling and pouring, but these words were not used in place of baptism for the remission of sins to be added by the Lord to the church.

Singing was without mechanical instrumental accompaniment

Mechanical instruments of music are not mentioned even one time in the worship of the New Testament church. There are ten passages that deal with the kind of music used, and all of them mention singing (Matthew 26:30; Mark 14:26; Acts 16:25; Romans 15:9; 1 Corinthians 14:15; Ephesians 5:19; Colossians 3:16; Hebrews 2:12; 13:15; James 5:13). If any of these passages *include* a mechanical instrument, then it would be *wrong* not to have it. And, we would *all have to play it*—for whatever these passages tell you to do, they tell me and everyone else to do!

The faith of its members was in Christ and His Word was their only guide

Write out and memorize, if you haven't already, John 3:16. _____
_____
_____

What did Paul affirm of the Scriptures in 2 Timothy 3:16-17? _____
_____
_____

What does 2 John 9 teach? _____
_____
_____

The word of Christ and the apostles whom He sent out as His personal representatives to reveal His will to men is the only rule of faith and practice for the one true church (John 12:48; Matthew 10:40).

The unity of the Spirit was the plea

How does the Psalmist describe unity in Psalm 133? _____
_____

For what does Jesus pray in John 17:20-21? _____
_____

What words express the unity of the early church in Acts 4:32? _____
_____
_____

List the seven ones of Ephesians 4:4-6. _____
_____
_____

When the church at Corinth had issues of division, Paul penned, "Now I plead with you, brethren, by the name of our Lord Jesus Christ, that you all speak the _____ _____, and that there be _____
_____ among you, but that you be perfectly _____
_____ in the _____ _____ and in the
_____ _____" (1 Corinthians 1:10).

These twelve characteristics are distinctive marks of the one true church. These same marks will characterize any church today, if that church is truly the church of Christ.

Some questions from our study

1. Write down and learn these 12 characteristics so well that you are able to cite them without looking. _____

    _____

    _____

    _____

    _____

2. Show from the Scriptures where and when the church was established.

    _____

    _____

    _____

3. In the space provided, draw a diagram depicting the simple, local, independent government of the church.

Apostasy from the One True Church

Nearly ever since the Lord placed man upon the Earth, he has been turning his back on God and His commands. This can happen on an individual basis for sure, but it can and does occur on a group, or congregational level as well. Each local church must keep and guard itself against doing this very thing.

Apostasy defined

The American Heritage Dictionary defines apostasy as "the abandonment of one's religious faith, a political party, one's principles, or a cause."

Anytime a person of God, or a group of believers desert God, it qualifies as apostasy. Sadly, God's people have been relinquishing their spiritual ways for a long time. Read and study the following texts. In the provided space, make a note of who apostatized and how.

1. Genesis 3:6-7 _____
   _____
   _____

2. Exodus 32:2-4 _____
   _____
   _____

3. Leviticus 10:1-2 _____
   _____
   _____

4. 2 Timothy 4:10 _____
   _____
   _____

Memory Verse

...Ask for the **old paths**, where the **good way** is, and **walk** in it; Then you will find **rest** for your **souls**.

- Jeremiah 6:16

Determining the cause of apostasy

The fact apostasy occurs is undeniable. It happens, and will continue to, as long as the earth stands. What is important to possess is the ability and knowledge to determine why and when apostasy occurs. Once this skill has been attained, apostasy will transpire less and less. Consider the following reasons why apostasy materializes.

1. When there is disrespect for authority, apostasy occurs.

    Authority in religion is vitally important. When there is disregard for authority, chaos is sure to reign. The book of Judges serves as a prime example for these very actions. "In those days there was no _____ in Israel; everyone did what was _____ in his own _____" (Judges 17:6, 21:25). When there is no plea for doing only authorized things, unapproved actions are sure to follow.

    The one true church must recognize Jesus as the One who has "_____ authority" (Matthew 28:18). Additionally, the one true church also recognizes the New Testament in its entirety constitutes the commands of the Lord. Paul penned, "If anyone thinks himself to be a prophet or spiritual, let him _____ that the things which I write to you are the _____ of the _____" (1 Corinthians 14:37).

2. When there is an attempt to change God's setup, apostasy occurs.

    For a very long time, man has been endeavoring to alter God's setup. This occurs as a result of not being satisfied with the

> In those days there was **no king** in Israel; everyone did what was **right** in his **own eyes**.
>
> - Judges 17:6

Lord's plan. There are three Old Testament occurrences which illustrate this sinful concept.

a. God had instituted a system of judges to be the leaders and deliverers of His people. This worked very well for awhile. Over time though, the children made a demand of Samuel, "Now make us a _____ to judge us like all the _____" (1 Samuel 8:5). This caused Samuel to feel as though he had been rejected, but God made it clear, "they have not _____ you, but they have rejected _____, that I should not reign over them" (1 Samuel 8:7).

> ...Now make us a **king** to **judge** us like all the **nations**.
>
> - 1 Samuel 8:5

b. Jeroboam became king of Israel (the northern kingdom) during the infancy of the Divided Kingdom. The children of Israel were commanded to go to Jerusalem (in the southern kingdom) at certain times of the year to fulfill their duties. However, Jeroboam said, "If these people go up to offer sacrifices in the house of the LORD at _____, then the heart of this people will turn _____ to their lord, Rehoboam king of Judah, and they will _____ me and go back to Rehoboam king of Judah" (1 Kings 12:27). Jeroboam "made two _____ of gold" (1 Kings 12:28) and instructed the people to worship them, one being in _____ and the other in _____ (1 Kings 12:29). This was considered a "_____," and was most certainly frowned upon by God (1 Kings 12:30).

c. The people of Jeremiah's day had gone their own way, doing their own things. The prophet tried to convince them to come back by saying "_____ in the ways and see, And ask for the old paths, where the good way is, And _____ in it; Then you will find _____ for your souls." Sadly, the people refused to return and said "We will not _____ in it" (Jeremiah 6:16).

The one true church is completely and wholly satisfied with God's set-up. It is, in no way, tempted to alter it.

3. When men agree to disagree, apostasy occurs.

Brethren are not always going to agree, and that is fine when it comes to matters of opinion. But when it comes to doctrinal matters (issues which God has already decided upon through His Word), there is no room for human opinion.

The fancy name for this false doctrine is "unity in diversity." It stems from men desiring to have their own thoughts and sentiments considered law.

The one true church has a burning desire to be unified. This can only arise as a congregation determines to use the Word of God as its unifying source. Look up the following passages and record what is said regarding unity.

a. Psalm 133:1 _____
_____
_____

b. 1 Corinthians 1:10 _____
_____
_____

Behold, how **good** and how **pleasant** it is for brethren to dwell together in **unity**!

- Psalm 133:1

    c.   Romans 12:16 _____

        _____

        _____

    d.   Proverbs 6:19_____

        _____

        _____

The one true church will always stand for the truth, and is concerned with teaching and practicing "the _____ counsel of _____" (Acts 20:27). The one true church refuses to compromise the truth simply in the name of "not getting into arguments."

4.   When Christians allow worldliness into their lives, apostasy occurs.

Even though God's people live "in" the world, they are not to be "of," or like the world. John warns, "Do not love the _____ or the things in the world" (1 John 2:15). In fact, Paul issued this command, "And do not be _____ to this _____, but be _____ by the renewing of your mind, that you may prove what is that good and acceptable and perfect will of God" (Romans 12:2).

The one true church not only teaches against worldliness, it works long, hard and diligently to be sure the world does not have an impact upon the Lord's body. Once worldliness is allowed in, individually or congregationally, it is highly difficult to remove.

Guarding against apostasy

It is imperative the one true church does all it can to protect and defend itself against abandoning God, His Word and His church. Paul does an excellent job in summing up the best way to do this. He wrote, "Therefore, my beloved brethren, be _____, _____, always abounding in the _____ of the Lord, knowing that your labor is not in _____ in the Lord" (1 Corinthians 15:58).

Be steady and consistent. Refuse to move off of God's plan. Work hard for the Lord. Doing these things will greatly minimize the possibility of apostasy.

Some questions from our study

1. What is the definition of apostasy? _____
    _____
    _____

2. How much authority does Christ have, and how much does that leave
    us? _____
    _____

3. How did Jeroboam change God's setup? _____
    _____
    _____

4. Write down the many different ways the "world" can make an impact on
    the church. _____
    _____
    _____
    _____
    _____

Denominationalism Versus the One True Church

According to statistics, there are approximately 30,000—40,000 different religious denominations spanning the globe. Yet, we read in the Bible there is "one body" (Ephesians 4:4), which is identified as the "church" (Colossians 1:18). This lesson is designed to identify the "marks" of denominationalism, and compare those to the one true church spoken of in the New Testament.

What is denominationalism?

By definition, denominationalism is "to separate into religious denominations," or "advocacy of separation into religious denominations," or "strict adherence to a denomination," or "sectarianism" (*American Heritage Dictionary*).

A "denomination" is a "break off" or "section" of something else. For example, 2 five dollar bills are denominations of a ten dollar bill, or 100 pennies are denominations of a one dollar bill. Religiously, a "denomination" is created when one religious group "breaks off" from another.

As an example of the basic definition of denomination, notice in Acts 5:17, there was a "_____ of the Sadducees" identified, just as there were a "_____ of the Pharisees" recognized in Acts 15:5. These groups, by definition, were denominations, or break offs of another, presumably larger group.

Memory Verse

Every **plant** which My heavenly Father has **not planted** will be **uprooted**.

- Matthew 15:13

When did denominations begin to occur?

For nearly 600 years, there was the Lord's church, and no other. Then, in 606 A.D., the Roman Catholic Church was officially formed. In 1517, Martin Luther nailed his 95 theses to the door of the Wittenberg Church in Germany, starting what is commonly referred to as the Protestant period. At this time, denominations began to rapidly appear. Notable ones such as Lutheran, Baptist, and Methodist were born in this era. From that point to the present, many different and varied denominations have been born.

Marks of denominationalism

The following "marks" and "signs" of denominationalism violate the pattern of the one true church set forth in the New Testament.

1. Denominationalism violates the New Testament's plea for unity.

    The authors of the New Testament made it clear regarding God's call for unity. God's plan is for His people to be united as "one." Look up the following verses and make a note of what is said with regard to unity.

    a. Acts 4:32 _____ _____

    b. Romans 12:16 _____ _____

    c. Romans 15:6 _____ _____

    d. 1 Corinthians 1:10 _____ _____

Be of the **same mind** toward one another.

- Romans 12:16a

e.   Philippians 3:16 _____

_____

f.   1 Peter 3:8 _____

_____

Even the Lord Himself in His prayer said, "I do not pray for these alone, but also for those who will _____ in Me through their word; that they all may be _____" (John 17:20-21).

The very reason for the formation of a denomination is disagreement with beliefs, teachings and doctrines of a religious group. Those who differ set out to "establish" a new denomination that better corresponds to their opinions.

With this information in mind, answer the following question: Is it possible to comply with the Bible's plea to be "one" when there are so many different religious groups (all of which teach and believe different things) in the world?

_____

2.   Denominationalism violates the New Testament's plea for self-government.

God clearly lays out His plan in Scripture for how the one true church governs itself. Each local church is to be "overseen" by _____ (1 Peter 5:1-3) and to be served by _____ (1 Timothy 3:8-13). Centralized and nationalized religious governments are a foreign concept to the Word of God.

Denominationalism disregards this call for autonomy (self-government) as it typically has national or world headquarters, along with annual gatherings of their leaders to determine its path and doctrine.

> I do not pray for these alone, but also for those who will **believe** in Me through their word; that **they all may be one**, as You, Father, are in Me, and I in You; that they also may be **one in Us**, that the world may **believe** that You sent Me.
>
> - John 17:20-21

For our **citizenship** is in **heaven**, from which we also **eagerly wait** for the Savior, the Lord Jesus Christ.

- Philippians 3:20

With this information in mind, answer the following question: Is it possible to be self-governed while at the same time have multiple levels of government nationally or globally?

_____

3. Denominationalism violates the New Testament's identification of the church's Head and Founder.

    The New Testament simply and clearly identifies the head of the one true church, "_____ is the _____ of the church" (Ephesians 5:23). Jesus is alive at the right hand of God, making the church's headquarters and our "_____...in heaven" (Philippians 3:20). The Lord's church will never be rendered headless.

    This cannot be said of denominations, most of which have a human head. When this human head passes away, and he will (Hebrews 9:27), that particular denomination will, for a space of time, be rendered headless.

    With this information in mind, answer the following question: Is it possible to have a human head and Jesus as the Head at the same time? _____

    Also, the Bible identifies Jesus as the founder of the one true church. The Son of God said, "on this _____, I will build My _____" (Matthew 16:18). It rightfully belongs to Him as He is the One who "_____ with His own _____" the church (Acts 20:28).

    Denominations, by their very nature, are founded by men. John and Charles Wesley founded the Methodist church while John Smyth founded the Baptist church. Charles Taze Russell founded the Jehovah's Witness religion, and Joseph Smith founded the Mormon church.

Unless these previously mentioned men died for the church, they are not and cannot be the head or the founder of the one true church. The one true church is of divine origin, not human.

With this information in mind, answer the following question: Is it possible for the one true church to have Jesus as its head and founder and also a man as its head and founder?_____

4. Denominationalism violates the New Testament's description of the church.

   It should be noted there is no "exclusive" name given for the one true church of the New Testament. However, it is described in several different ways. Examine the following verses and write down the description of the church.

   a. Romans 14:17 _____
   _____
   _____

   b. Romans 16:16 _____
   _____
   _____

   c. 1 Corinthians 1:2 _____
   _____
   _____

   d. 1 Timothy 3:15_____
   _____
   _____

For the **kingdom** of God is not **eating** and **drinking**, but **righteousness** and **peace** and **joy** in the Holy Spirit.

- Romans 14:17

It is important to understand why the one true church is described as the "Church of Christ." The best way to do this is to break down this three-word phrase. Consider.

"Church" is defined as "out of." The church is a collection of people who have been "called out" of the world "into" a relationship with God.

"Of" is important, as it signifies possession. For instance, Tallahassee is the capital "of" Florida, meaning that particular city belongs to Florida.

"Christ" is the Son of God, the King of Kings, the one who died and shed His blood to purchase the church (Acts 20:28).

When fully assembled, "Church of Christ" describes a group of people who have been called out of the world and belong to Jesus, the Christ.

This stands in contrast to denominations, whose names and descriptions offer no glory to Christ, or who have no rooting in the Bible. Some denominations bear the name of their founder (Lutheran and Wesleyan for example). Other denominations use actions or ways of their religion (Baptist and Methodist for example).

With this information in mind, answer the following question. Is it possible or right for the one true church to believe that Jesus died for it yet describe it in unbiblical ways? _____

Is the one true church a denomination?

Often this question is posed, and it is certainly worthy of an answer. The answer is no, it is not a denomination. Why? Because it is not a "break off" or "sect" of any other religious group. It is the one true church established on the day of Pentecost in Acts 2.

Today, those who desire to become members of this church do so in the same exact way as those in Acts 2. Present members of the one true church worship and behave in the same ways as the church in the New Testament (Acts 2:42; 20:7). Present members of the one true church describe themselves in the same way the church in the New Testament did (Romans 16:16). Those who desire to please God and obey Him must seek out this church and become part of it. Will you?

Some questions from our study

1. What is the definition of a denomination? _____
    _____
    _____

2. Explain, in your own words, what Jesus meant when he prayed for His
    people to be "one." _____
    _____
    _____

3. Fill in the blanks. Each local church is to be overseen by
    _____ and served by _____. The head of the
    church is _____, and the headquarters of the church is in
    _____.

4. List some Biblical descriptions of the one true church. _____
    _____
    _____
    _____

5. Describe, in your own words, why the one true church is not a
    denomination. _____
    _____
    _____
    _____

Restoring the One True Church

Once a local body of believers has fallen away, being involved in unauthorized teaching and practice, it is imperative it finds its way back. Two books in the Old Testament provide an excellent blueprint for "restoration"—Ezra and Nehemiah. These noble men led scores of Jews back to Jerusalem to restore the place and ways of worship. Embedded within the pages of these books are the ways men today will plot their way back to God.

Step 1: Realization of the problem

It has been true for all time—no problem will be solved until it is first recognized as an issue. In Nehemiah 1:3 it was reported, "The survivors who are left from the captivity in the province are there in great _____ and reproach. The _____ of Jerusalem is also broken _____, and its gates are _____ with fire."

We, too, must be aware of the issues facing the one true church. Read Revelation 3:17. In what three ways did the Laodicean brethren see themselves?

1. _____

   _____

2. _____

   _____

3. _____

   _____

Memory Verse

Remember therefore from where you have **fallen**; **repent** and do the **first works**, or else I will come to you quickly and **remove** your lampstand from its place—unless you **repent**.

- Revelation 2:5

However, Jesus made it clear they had a false impression of themselves. In other words, they did not realize there was an issue. Jesus described them in five ways. What were they?

1. _____

_____

2. _____

_____

3. _____

_____

4. _____

_____

5. _____

_____

Examine yourselves as to whether you are in the **faith**. **Test** yourselves. Do you not know yourselves, that **Jesus Christ** is in you?—unless indeed you are **disqualified**.

- 2 Corinthians 13:5

Individual children of God and local bodies of believers would do very well to obey Paul's command to "_____ yourselves as to whether you are in the faith. _____ yourselves" (2 Corinthians 13:5).

Step 2: Proper sorrow over the problem

Once admittance of the issue has been made, appropriate sorrow should follow. If there is none, then restoration is not possible. Upon hearing the news about the state of Jerusalem's wall, Nehemiah "sat down and _____, and _____ for many days; I was fasting and praying before the God of heaven" (Nehemiah 1:4). His sadness was apparent even to the king who asked "Why is your face _____, since you are not sick? This is nothing but sorrow of _____" (Nehemiah 2:2).

When we realize we have fallen away, true and genuine sorrow must occur. Paul speaks of two kinds of sorrow, and where they each lead in 2 Corinthians 7:9-10. Make a note of this information in the space below.

1. _____

_____

2. _____

_____

Step 3: Hard work

There is no substitute for hard and determined work. Nothing can take its place. The ways of worship and the wall of Jerusalem were not restored without it. It is reported that the folks of Ezra's group would "strengthen their _____ in the _____ of the house of God, the God of Israel" (Ezra 6:22). Those who traveled with Nehemiah were no less determined. Search the following verses, and report what they have to say about the Jews' work.

1. Nehemiah 2:18_____

_____

2. Nehemiah 4:6_____

_____

These good people worked so hard, they were able to finish restoring the wall in just _____ days (Nehemiah 6:15).

When it is discovered the one true church is in need of restoration, hard and untiring labor is necessary. Paul said it this way, "Therefore, my beloved brethren, be _____, immovable, always abounding in the _____ of the Lord, knowing that your labor is not in _____ in the Lord" (1 Corinthians 15:58).

People of God who are interested in restoration and in pleasing the Almighty are not afraid of work. They relish the opportunity to be busy for God.

So we built the wall, and the **entire wall** was joined together up to half its height, for the people had a **mind to work**.

- Nehemiah 4:6

Step 4: Diligence

> Whatever is **commanded** by the God of heaven, let it **diligently** be done for the house of the **God of heaven**.
>
> - Ezra 7:23a

Those who are charting a return to God must be people of diligence. "Diligence" is a tireless persistence in the pursuit of a goal. In his address to God's people Ezra said, "Whatever is _____ by the God of heaven, let it _____ be _____ for the house of the God of heaven" (Ezra 7:23).

Too often, folks give up, give in and quit when the going gets rough. Restoring the one true church is hard work, and quitting is not an option. Investigate the following verses and write down what they say about diligence.

1.   2 Peter 1:5,10 _____

_____

_____

2.   Deuteronomy 4:9; 6:7 _____

_____

_____

3.   Psalm 119:4 _____

_____

_____

4.   Luke 15:8_____

_____

_____

Those who wish to restore must abide by the words of the Hebrew writer: "But without faith it is _____ to please Him, for he who comes to God must _____ that He is, and that He is a rewarder of those who _____ seek Him" (Hebrews 11:6).

Step 5: Prayer

Successful restorers are people of prayer. They effectively and consistently communicate with God.

It is noted that "Ezra was _____" (Ezra 10:1). As well, Nehemiah was a praying man. Below, draw a line from the verse on the left to the proper description of the prayer on the right.

Nehemiah 1:11	Prayer at reception of bad news
Nehemiah 4:9	Prayer for mercy
Nehemiah 1:4	Prayer to help deal with trouble
Nehemiah 2:4	Prayer of confession
Nehemiah 1:6	Telling others about his prayer life

Today, those who attempt to help restore the one true church need to be prayerful. The Bible is abounding with admonitions to pray.

In Acts 1:24, the eleven remaining apostles "_____" as they selected an apostle to replace Judas Iscariot. When important work is to be done, like restoring, it is imperative prayer be made.

In Acts 20:36, as Paul was offering a goodbye to the Ephesian elders, it says "he knelt down and _____ with them all." Under great times of stress, often occurring during times of restoration, prayer is mandatory.

Never forget to pray. Without it, successful restoration is simply not possible.

Step 6: Unity and cooperation

It is clear Ezra and Nehemiah were successful as a result of the unity and cooperation of the people. Though there were scores of people present, it is written the "_____ gathered together as _____ man to Jerusalem" (Ezra 3:1). The same is said in Nehemiah 8:1 as "the _____ gathered together as _____ man in the open square."

When a restoration attempt is underway, people must be unified and cooperative as the work progresses. Unity is a pleasing thing to God. Locate the following verses and note what they have to say about being unified.

1. Psalm 133:1 _____

_____

2.   Ephesians 4:3 _____
     _____

It is nearly impossible to do important spiritual work while seeds of discord are being sown. Remember, God hates "one who sows _____ among brethren" (Proverbs 6:19).

Step 7: Plea for the Word of God

If restoration is to take place, it will occur on the foundation of God's Word. Ezra and Nehemiah made it a point to focus the people's attention on God's law. Ezra did "as it is _____ in the Law of Moses" (Ezra 3:2). He "had _____ his heart to seek the _____ of the LORD" (Ezra 7:10).

The people wanted Ezra "to bring the Book of the _____ of Moses, which the LORD had _____ Israel" (Nehemiah 8:1). Ezra "read _____ from the book, in the _____ of God; and they gave the sense, and helped them to _____ the reading" (Nehemiah 8:8).

Restoration of the one true church will not occur until God's Word becomes the only source of authority.

Restoration is possible...and needful

In too many places, the church has involved itself in practices and teachings which are not God-authorized. This can be reversed by those who identify and properly sorrow about the problem. This situation can be fixed by hard work, diligence, prayer and unity. When the Word of God becomes champion, restoration is right around the corner.

Some questions from our study

1.   List the two sorrows spoken of in 2 Corinthians 7:9-10. What is the difference between the two? _____
     _____
     _____

2.   Why is prayer so important in restoring? _____
     _____
     _____

3. In your own words, explain why diligence is needed in restoring. _____

    _____

    _____

    _____

Made in the USA
Columbia, SC
01 September 2024

40881436R00055